A Math Skills Book to Stretch Your Brain

Copyright © 2005 by innovativeKids®
18 Ann Street, Norwalk, CT 06854
www.innovativekids.com
ZB Font Method Copyright © 1996 Zaner-Bloser

ONE FISHY SCHOOL

What color are the fish in the kindergarten fish tank? Find out!
Color the fish by following the numbers and colors below.

| 1 = blue | 2 = yellow | 3 = purple |
| 4 = red | 5 = green | 6 = orange |

EXTRA! EXTRA! • Trace all the numbers from 1 to 6 above. Next, draw a big fish and write the number 7 in it. Draw a small fish and write the number 8 in it. Now find the fish that tells how old you are. Give it a special hat!

FISH FINDER

The kids are going fishing. Can you help them find the fish?
Color each space to make the fish appear.

| 1 = blue | 2 = orange | 3 = purple |
| 4 = brown | 5 = green | 6 = red |

EXTRA! EXTRA! • How many purple fish do you count in the picture? • How many boats? • How many red fish? • How many green leaves? • How many children? • One fish is not colored in. Color it your favorite color!

PLAY BALL!

These ballplayers need to find their gloves!
Look at the gloves near each player.
Color the glove that has the same number as the player's shirt.

EXTRA! EXTRA! • Find players 1, 3, and 5. Color their shirts red! Find players 2 and 4. Color their shirts purple. • Which team has more players, red or purple? • Which team should you join to make the teams even? Draw yourself in baseball clothes that are the right color.

DO FEED THE SQUIRRELS!

Help the hungry squirrels find their acorns! Look at the numbers on each squirrel's shirt, and follow the path with that number. Count the acorns that are waiting at the end!

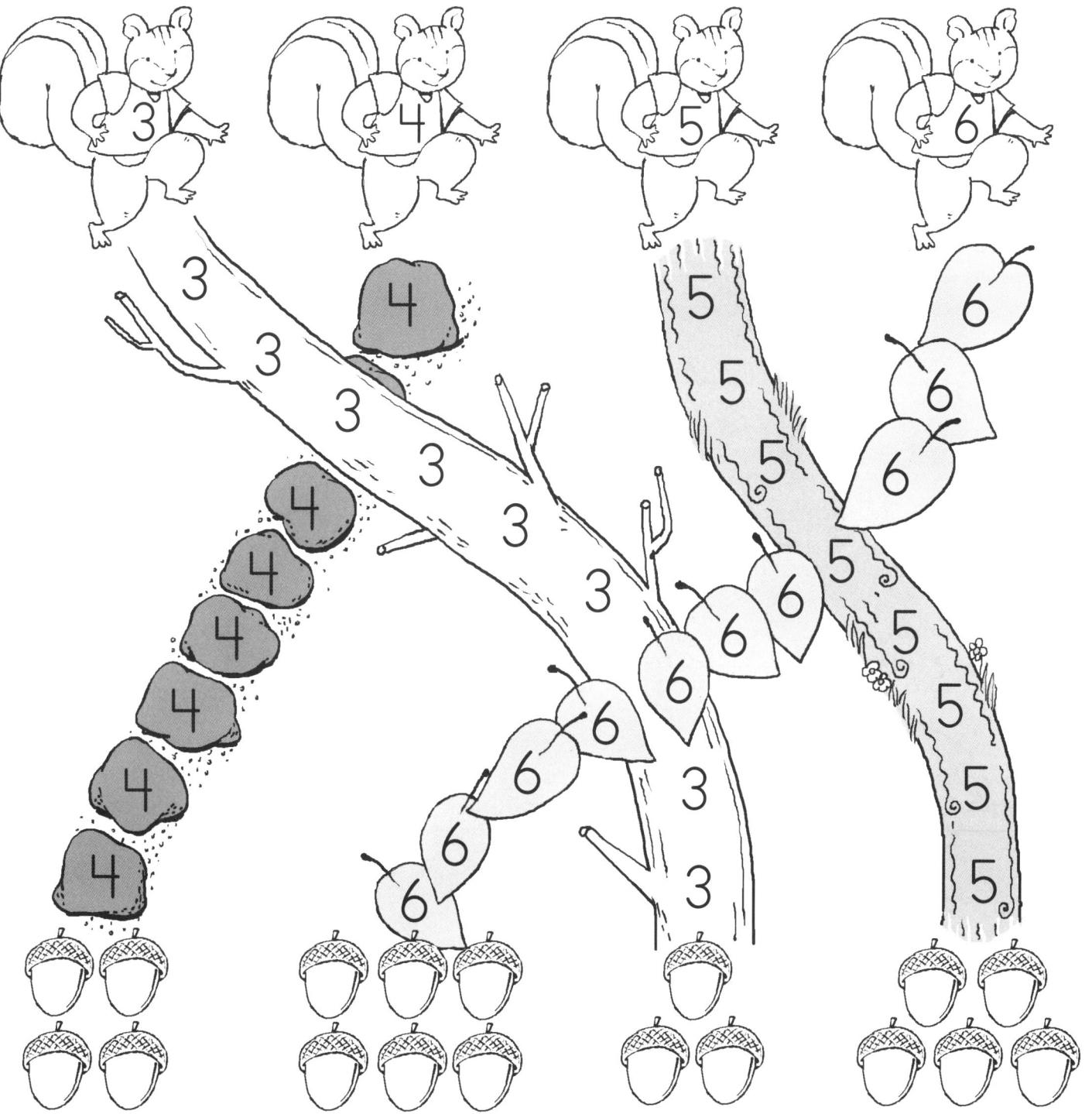

EXTRA! EXTRA! • Which squirrel got the biggest number of acorns? Color its shirt green. Which squirrel got the smallest number of acorns? Color its shirt yellow. How many acorns did those two squirrels get all together?

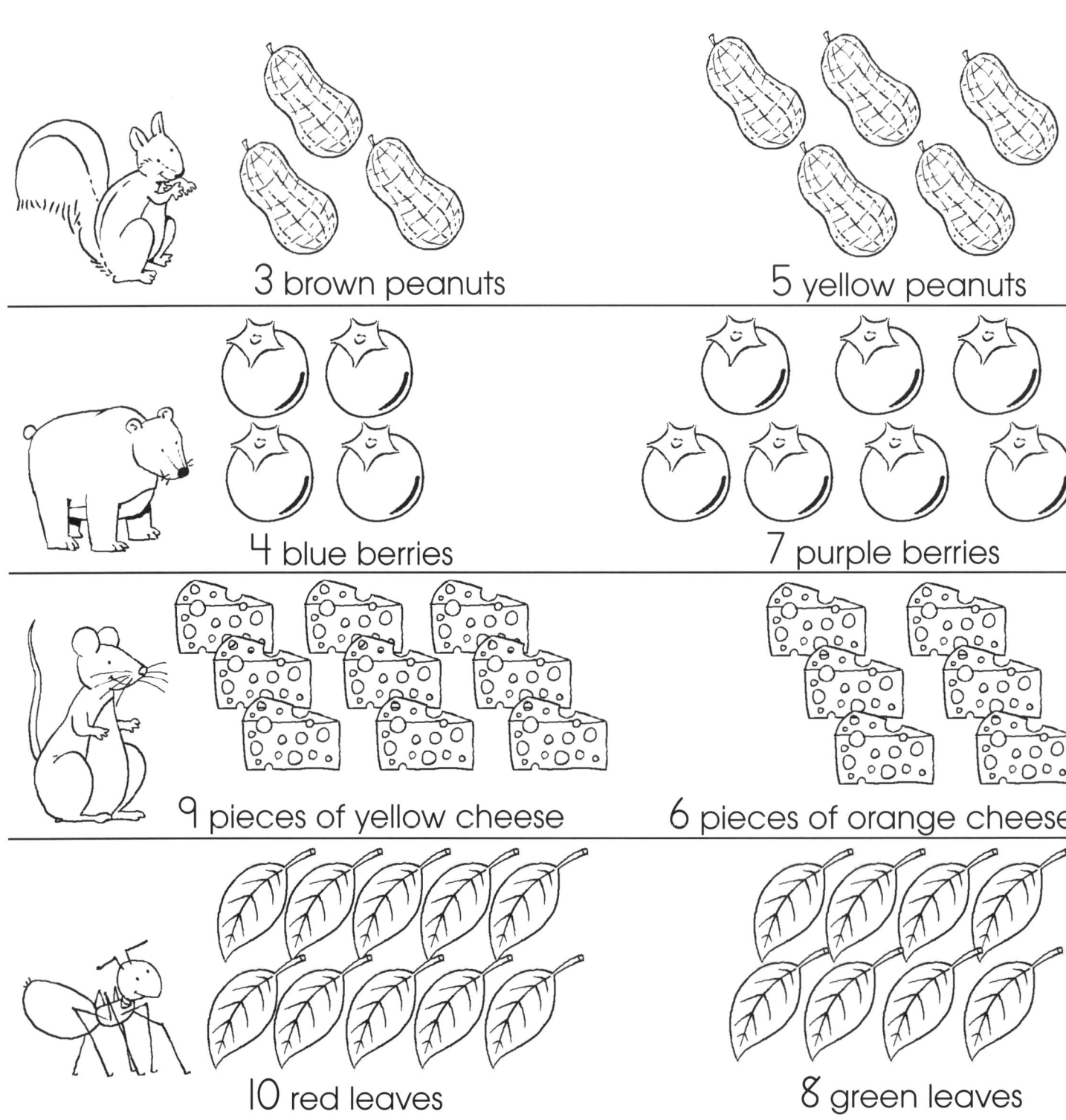

ART SMARTS

It is time for art class! Count the class art supplies in each group.
Then trace the correct number.

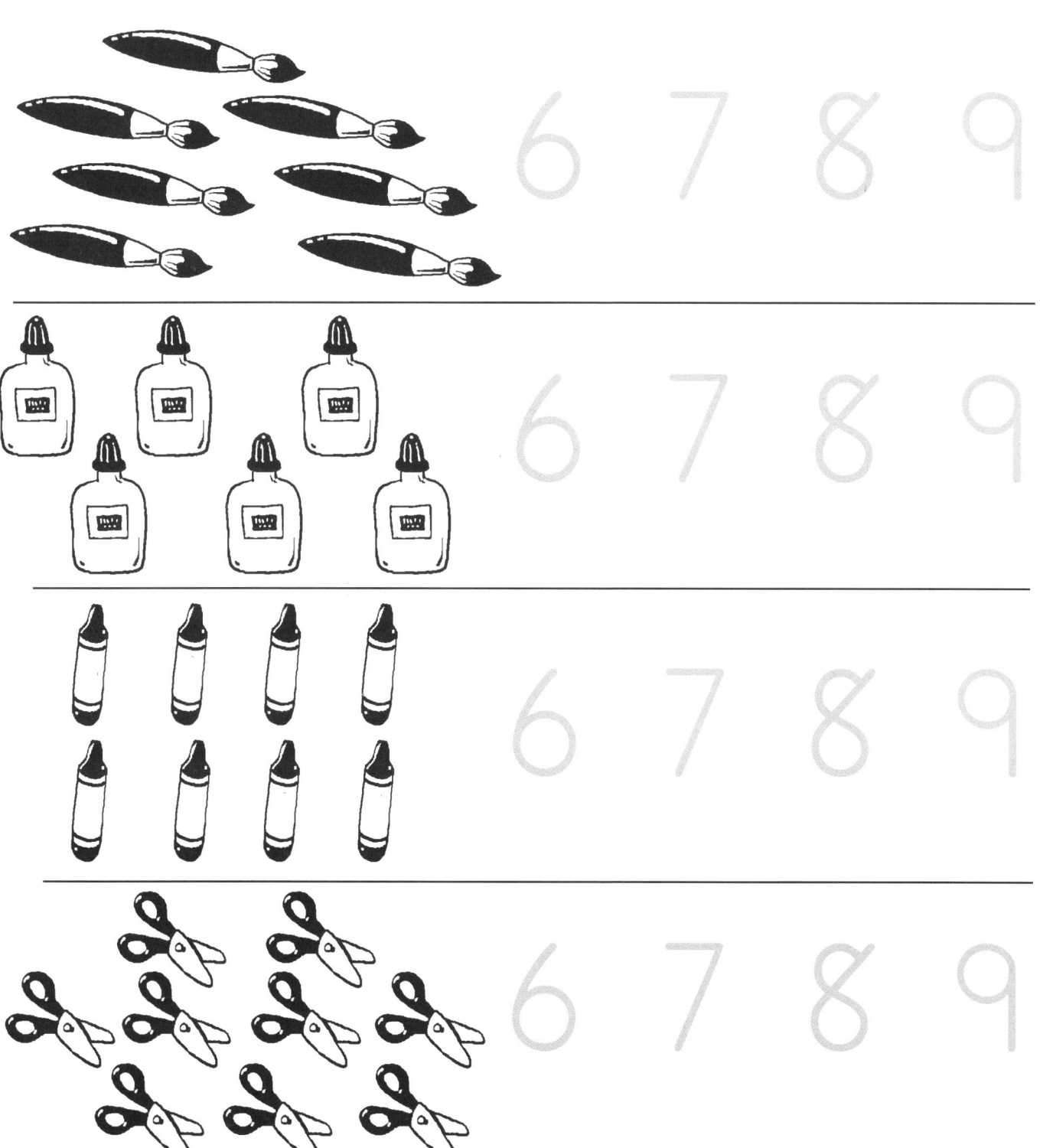

EXTRA! EXTRA! • Which group has the biggest number of art supplies? Draw a circle around that group. • Which group has the smallest number of art supplies? Draw a rectangle around that group.

READY, SET, DRAW!

This kindergarten class likes to draw. Look at their great drawings! You can help color them.

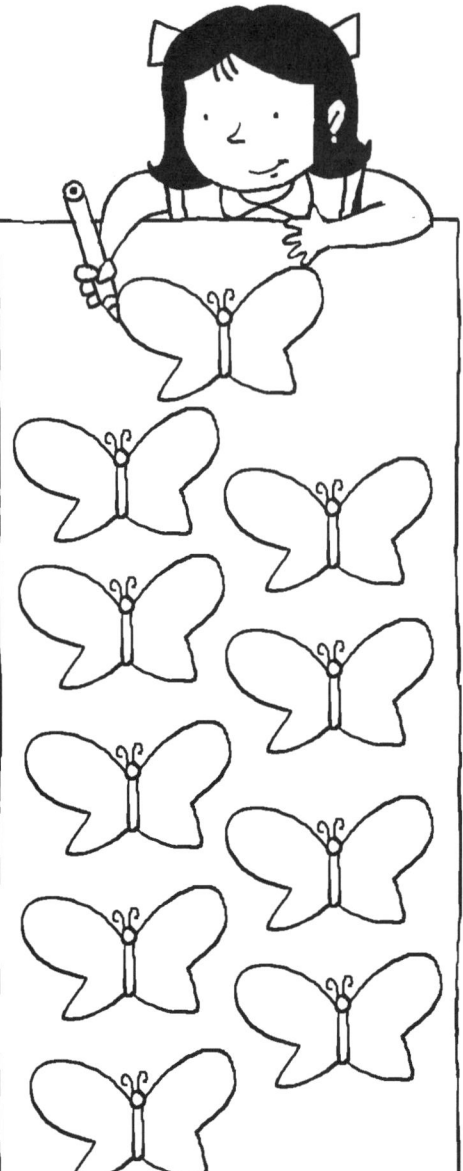

Color 6 cars the color of the sky during the day.

Color 4 cars the color of a dark night sky.

Color 5 butterflies the color of a lemon.

Color 5 butterflies the color of grape juice.

Color 8 frogs the color of grass.

Color 2 frogs the color of dirt.

<u>EXTRA! EXTRA!</u> • Count all the cars. How many are there? Now count all the butterflies and all the frogs. How many of each thing are there?

A HORSE RACE!

Which horse is first? Trace the number 1 below him.
Which horse is second? Trace the number 2 below him.
Which horse is third? Trace the number 3 below him.

EXTRA! EXTRA! • The judges have prizes for the horses. Color the trophy yellow, and write the number 1 on it. Color the ribbon red and write the number 2 on it. Color the certificate orange and write the number 3 on it. Color each horse to match the prize it will get.

TREASURE!

Look what the explorer found! Count each kind of treasure. On the treasure list, write the number that says how many.

How many?

_____

_____

_____

_____

_____

_____

<u>Extra! Extra!</u> • What did the explorers find the most of? What did the explorers find the least of? What treasure could you use to buy something with? What two kinds of treasure are things you can wear? • What kind of treasure would you like to find? Where would you look?

SPACE COUNT!

What does the astronaut see in space?
Count the objects in each group. Draw a line to match each group of objects with the number that says how many.

2

5

4

10

7

1

Extra! Extra! • Draw a triangle around the number that says how many legs the astronaut has.
• Draw a square around the number that says how many legs each alien has. • Circle the number that says how many points each star has.

JUNGLE JUMBLE!

Answer the questions and write the numbers.

How many bananas?   How many bananas?

_____   _____

Color the monkey that has more bananas.

How many birds?   How many birds?

_____   _____

Color the tree that has less birds.

 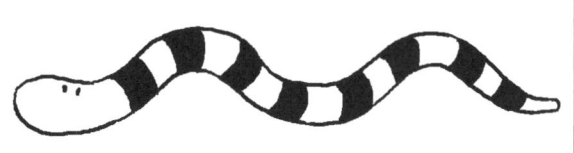 

How many black stripes?   How many black stripes?   How many black stripes?

_____   _____   _____

Color the two snakes that have the same number of stripes.

EXTRA! EXTRA! • Color the biggest banana in each bunch brown. Color the smallest banana in each bunch green. • Give the longest snake a smile. Give the shortest snake a long tongue. • Write the first letter of your first name on the shorter tree!

MATH MYSTERY!

The kindergarten class got a new pet! It squeaks and it likes cheese.
Connect the numbers in order from 1 to 10 to see it.

EXTRA! EXTRA! • Can you draw ten more holes in the piece of cheese? Count out loud while you draw them. • Put your finger on the number 10 in the dot to dot. Can you count backwards? Try it: 10 9 8 7 6 5 4 3 2 1.

GROW, GARDEN, GROW!

The kindergartners planted a garden in the school yard!
Read the questions below and trace the correct answers.

How many pumpkins?
1 2 3 4 5

Draw 1 more.

How many now?
1 2 3 4 5

How many cucumbers?
1 2 3 4 5

Draw 2 more.

How many now?
1 2 3 4 5

How many tomatoes?
1 2 3 4 5

Draw 3 more.

How many now?
1 2 3 4 5

EXTRA! EXTRA! • It is time to pick the vegetables! Cross out 1 pumpkin. How many are left?
• Cross out 2 tomatoes. How many are left? • Cross out 2 cucumbers. How many are left?
• What colors are pumpkins, tomatoes, and cucumbers? Color them!

SCHOOL'S OUT!

What can you count?

How many windows? _____   How many kids? _____

How many books? _____   How many mittens? _____

How many buttons? _____   How many balls? _____

EXTRA! EXTRA! • Draw a square lunch box for the boy who has buttons. • Draw a rectangle-shaped lunch box for the girl with three balls. • Draw a circle-shaped sun in the sky. • Now draw yourself somewhere in the picture!

THE BUS RUSH!

Can you help these buses get home? Write in the missing numbers along each road to help them get where they are going.

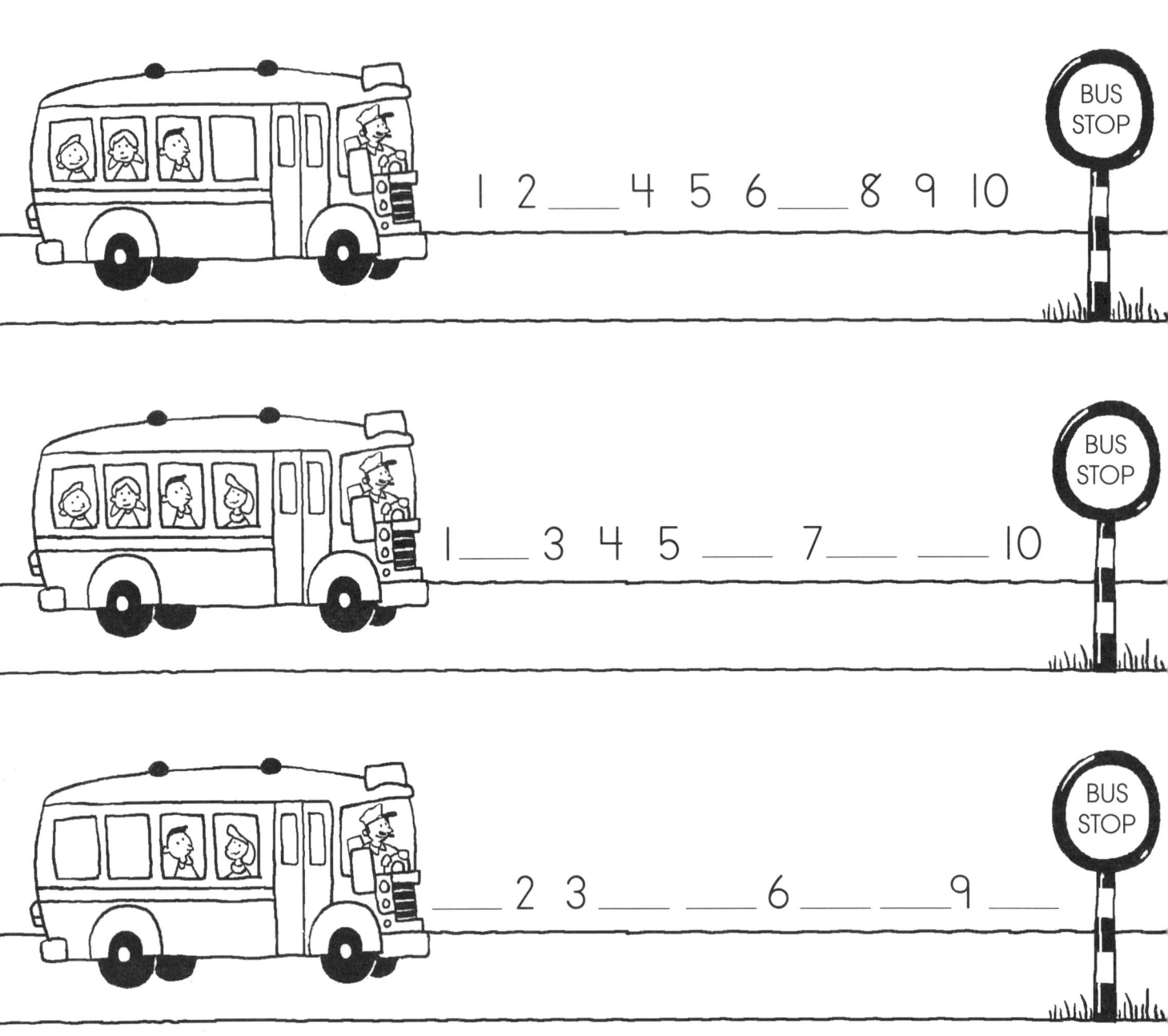

EXTRA! EXTRA! • How many kids are on the top bus? Draw one puppy at the bus stop for each kid. How many kids are on the middle bus? Draw one flower at the bus stop for each kid. How many kids are on the bottom bus? Draw one mom or dad at the bus stop for each kid.